COMPUTERS FOR KIDS

COMPUTERS FOR KIDS

Chris Cataldo

authorHOUSE®

AuthorHouse™
1663 Liberty Drive
Bloomington, IN 47403
www.authorhouse.com
Phone: 1-800-839-8640

Published by AuthorHouse   09/04/2012

ISBN: 978-1-4772-6659-5 (sc)
ISBN: 978-1-4772-6657-1 (hc)
ISBN: 978-1-4772-6658-8 (e)

Library of Congress Control Number: 2012916319

<u>Who Is This Book For?</u>

This book is for kids who want to learn the computer at an early age. This book is generally intended for children around the age of 7. The book teaches the child the very basics of the computer. It also gives a very basic but yet strong foundation in getting to know the Microsoft Windows operating system.

How The Book Is Designed

The book is designed as a very graphic way to teach children the computer. I believe that a child learns best if he/she can associate a picture with a word. The chapters are very small so the child can pick up on the material fairly quickly. It is meant to be a fun way to learn as well.

LEGAL STUFF

Computers For Kids contains images and logos that I have received written permission by the companies who own them.

Microsoft Windows is a registered trademark of Microsoft Corporation in the United States and other countries.

DEDICATIONS

This book is dedicated to the following people (in no special order).

William: A fellow author who inspired me to start this book. If I didn't have food delivered, we would have never met and this book would have probably not have been born. Thank you for your support.

My Mom: You always told me as a kid to not let my vision get in the way of anything and that I can do anything I wanted, so, here I am writing this book.

My Wife: You helped me with proofreading and modifying this book. I realize I was probably a pain in the butt, but I want you to know that I really appreciate you helping me along the way.

Dr. Kestin: We've known each other for many years now and you are amazing. We've had some rough times along the way but whenever it came to my eyes, you were there. Without them, I wouldn't be able to do this book. Thank you for all your support.

Chris Cataldo

Friends: Thank you all for your support. You all have given me ideas and suggestions in the book and I have tried to use them in any way I could.

YOU, the child, who is reading this book and learning about the computer. Always learn as much as you can. Knowledge doesn't go bad and you can always gain more of it. Thank you for purchasing my book and I hope you enjoy it.

Table of Contents

CHAPTER 1

The Desktop Computer

The desktop computer is made up of 4 major parts. All these parts eventually connect together and talk to each other. We will talk about the parts of the computer now.

From this point on we will give these parts a new name. We will call them "devices". You will see why very soon.

The first "device" that a computer is made up of is called the **CPU**. This is better known as the "Central Processing Unit". This is the "box" that may be on the floor or on top of a desk.

The CPU looks similar to this:

The next device is known as the keyboard. A keyboard looks like this:

A keyboard is known as an input device to the computer. In other words, you give the computer instructions by entering commands in from the keyboard. A keyboard has letters, numbers, and symbols on it. It also has a number pad if you want to enter in numbers like a calculator.

Another feature of the keyboard is the function keys. These are at the top of the keyboard labeled as F1, F2, F3 etc. The function of these keys varies. On some machines they are used to turn the sound on and off. Other functions of these keys can be used for turning the wireless card on or off.

There are 3 types of keyboard connectors. One of them is very rarely used but is worth mentioning here. The three types of connectors are:

- A PS/2 connection

- A USB connection

- A wireless connection

For now, you don't need to know what the actual terms mean, just be familiar with how they look.

PS/2 connection:

USB connection:

Wireless:

Next in line is the screen part. Well it's actually not called that. The correct name for it is the *monitor*. The monitor is what is known as an output device as it displays information to you. A monitor looks like this:

Monitors come in all different sizes. The common size nowadays is between 17 and 21 inches wide as in the picture above. Years ago the monitors were more square than a rectangle. Just like keyboards, the monitors have 2 types of connections.

Here they are:

- 15-pin D connection

- HDMI connection

You can buy just the monitor cable if it gets lost or if some of the pins are damaged on the cable. You can also buy special cables that go from a 15 pin D connection to an HDMI connection. Most systems today come with an HDMI connection but be aware they may be using or have the option of the older 15 pin D connector.

Next, is the mouse. A mouse is considered an input device because you move it to tell the computer what to access. A mouse looks like this:

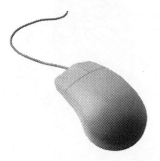

A mouse has three different types of connections. You have seen them with the keyboards. Yes, you guessed it, a PS/2 connection, USB connection and a wireless connection.

There are also different types of mice. The older type is a 3 button mouse and the newer ones are a 2 button mouse.

The difference in these types of mice is that the middle button on the 3 button mouse acts like a double click option. When you "double click" on something it usually opens up a program that you wanted to use on your computer.

You can also "left click" or "right click". If you "left click" once you are just highlighting the item. There is no further action. If you "right click" on something, depending on what it is, you will see another menu that will come up with a bunch of choices that you can choose from.

SUMMARY

- There are 3 types of connections for keyboards and mice. They are PS/2, USB and wireless connections.

- There are 2 types of connections for monitors. They are 15 pin D and HDMI connections.

Exercise 1: Next to each picture, write what it is.

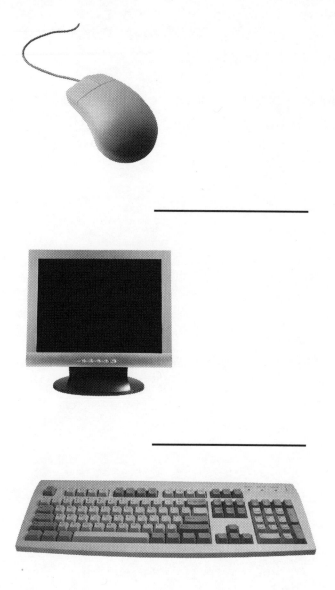

_____

_____

_____

If you need to go over this section, please do so now before moving on to the next section as this chapter will be a foundation for future chapters.

CHAPTER 2

What is in the "box"?

The "box" is made up of a lot of different components. Each component has its own functions but yet work with each other to make the overall functionality of the computer to work properly.

We will start with one of the most important items that is built into a computer. This part is known as the "motherboard" The motherboard holds many important components of the system. It provides many different types of connectors for other devices that you may have. A motherboard generally looks like this:

The motherboard consists of a few important components. They are as follows:

- CPU—Central Processing Unit

- Memory Slots

- Hard drive connectors

- USB ports

- Power supply

- Expansion Slots

Each of these components work together to perform input and output functions. Some of these perform both types of functions. We will look at each of these items in greater detail over the next several pages.

Motherboards come in different sizes. The size depends on the actual size of the computer case. I personally prefer a bigger case since the computer will have more ventilation and the system will not overheat as much. We will talk about this later when we talk about the power supply and its connections and functions. One of the downfalls about a motherboard is if any of the components go bad, such as a PCI slot or a chip, you may need to replace the entire motherboard. In most cases, this can be a couple hundred dollars. For a little more money, you can go out and get a new PC. A new PC nowadays will cost you around $600.

If the CPU, memory, or secondary video card goes bad, you can usually just replace those instead of going out and buying a whole new PC. These items will cost you much less and may fix your problems.

The CPU: Central Processing Unit

The CPU is basically the heart of the computer. Without a CPU the computer would not be functional. CPUs come in many different speeds. Today's systems usually come with a 3.0GHZ (Gigahertz) speed CPU. Years ago, CPUs were measured in MHZ (Megahertz). A CPU looks something like this:

The CPU is consisted of pins and grooves that fit perfectly onto the motherboard. Usually when you buy a CPU, you also purchase the motherboard that will go with it.

Memory

There are two kinds of memory. They are as follows:

• RAM—Read Access Memory

• ROM—Read Only Memory

RAM: This stands for Read Access Memory. This type of memory gets wiped out when you turn your computer off. Anything that you were working on will need to be saved to the computer's hard drive. If you do not do this, any data will be lost when the computer is turned off, whether you turned it off or by an accident, for example, the power plug was taken out of the wall. Just like with speeds on a CPU, RAM chips also have sped. RAM can be rewritten to. A RAM chip looks something like this:

ROM: This stands for Read Only Memory. This type of memory chip is inside the computer that is pre-programmed. The information that is stored on these chips are used for the operating system (Windows) and any hardware that needs to communicate with the software that is installed. A ROM chip looks something like this:

ROM chips are permanently mounted on the motherboard by the manufacturer and cannot be removed. The most common user interaction with a ROM chip is usually a BIOS (Basic Input Output System) update where a user would download an executable file to their desktop and run it.

Hard Drive Connectors

There are two main types of hard drive connections that you will find on a motherboard:

- IDE

- SATA

Here's what each of the two connections looks like:

IDE

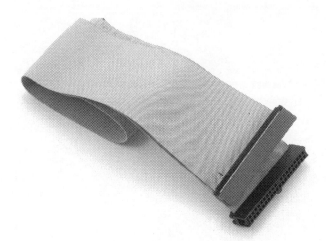

SATA

Some differences between IDE and SATA connections are as follows:

- IDE connections are usually slower in speed and performance than SATA.

- The IDE uses 40/80 pins to connect to a device. The SATA interface is much smaller.

These are the 2 most common differences between IDE and SATA.

Some devices that get connected via these technologies are hard drives and CD/DVD drives. If you were going to purchase a device for your PC, you need to make sure that the connection type is physically available and that you have room to plug in another device. You cannot use a SATA drive on an IDE connection. They are two different connection types and will not work on any PC.

Generally speaking, in today's world, you will only find the SATA type connection as the IDE is an older technology found in most PC's older than the year 2003. As of 2009, SATA has replaced approximately 99% of all IDE connections in consumer PC's.

USB Slots and Connectors

A USB port is today's most common way to connect computer peripherals along with mobile devices such as cell phones and iPads.

A USB port looks like this:

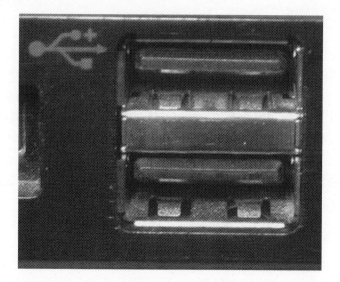

USB ports, just like other components in the computer, are measured at speeds. The older computers used to run USB 1.0. Today, most PC's are running USB 2.0. More and more PC's are now starting to come out with USB 3.0.

Here's the tricky part—Let's say you purchase a USB hard drive at your local store and it is USB 2.0 but your computer only has USB 3.0 ports. Will this device work on your computer? The answer is "YES". Here is why. When you connect a slower device to a higher speed port, the port drops it's speed to match that of the device. By doing this however, it may cause a bottleneck in the system and may cause the system to run a little slower.

Now if we take it the other way, where we purchased a USB 3.0 device and put it into a USB 2.0 port, the port will run at maximum speed but the device will not. You will get a message on the screen stating that the device could run faster and to try a different USB port.

Some devices that can be connected to a PC via USB are:

- Printers

- Scanners

- External Hard Drives

- Mouse

- Keyboard

The Power Supply

The power supply is a crucial part of the system. If there were no power supply, the computer would not even turn on. A power supply looks like this:

As you can see, there are black, yellow and red plugs coming out of it. These plugs are all connected to a power connector that looks like this:

Power supplies come in different sizes. You must look at your motherboard and case layout to determine which power supply is good for you. Once you determine the type of power supply you need then you can take a look at what components you might put inside the computer. Power supplies range in different wattage amounts and if you get the wrong wattage for your computer, you may cause damage to your motherboard and possibly burn it out and need to purchase a new one. Sometimes it can also do damage to other peripherals inside the computer such as the hard drive.

Power supplies also come with a built in fan to help cool the system. If the power supply fan stops working, there is a chance that the system will overheat and then not work correctly. Some symptoms of power supply failure are:

- Computer lockups

- The computer randomly shuts down

- Overheating issues

Always keep the power supply fan clear of any dirt or dust as this will prevent hot air from flowing outside of the PC and keeping the system cool at all times. I prefer a bigger desktop case as opposed to the mini towers. The bigger cases leave room for the PC to ventilate easier and more quickly.

Expansion Slots

Expansion slots are used for many different things. There are a few different types of expansion slots that you may find on your motherboard. They are as follows:

- PCI Express or better known as PCIe

- Conventional PCI

- AGP

- ISA

Let's take a little closer look at what each of these slots supports.

PCI Express

PCIe supports bandwidth speeds from 250MB/Sec to 8000MB/Sec. PCIe comes in different bus speeds—x1, x2, x4, x8, x16 and x32. These are basically known as "lanes" to transfer data. PCIe is also backwards compatible as it will work with older PCI cards. The PCI express slots can be different colors. These may represent the speeds of each slot if you have more than one. Please read your motherboard manual for further details. These are generally 64-bit slots.

Conventional PCI

A standard PCI slot is a bit slower in speeds. The speed of a conventional PCI slot is 132MB/Sec. These slots are typically white in color. They look similar to this:

AGP

AGP stands for Accelerated Graphics Port. This comes in 4 different modes or speeds. They are 1x, 2x, 4x and 8x. AGP cards are usually used for video display devices, such as a monitor. Some AGP cards come with a DVI connector so you can view your computer screen on a TV. These slots are typically a tan color.

Here is what an AGP expansion slot looks like:

ISA

ISA stands for Industry Standard Architecture. You will not see these types of expansion slots in any PC today. These types of slots are more than 30 years old. They first came out in 1981. They came in 8-bit and 16-bit modes. Later on, this turned into EISA—Extended Industry Standard Architecture.

Any older ISA expansion cards that you had would work in an EISA expansion slot. This is what is known as being "backward compatible". At last, the 32-bit slot was born.

An ISA slot looks similar to this:

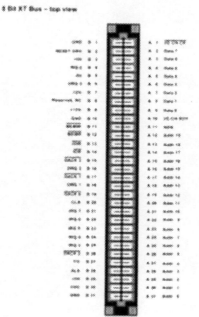

SUMMARY:

- The motherboard is consisted up of multiple components. These components work together to make the computer function.

- There are 2 kinds of memory. RAM—Random Access Memory and ROM—Read Only Memory

- There are 2 kinds of hard drive connections. They are IDE and SATA.

- The power supply is one of the most important components in the computer. Without it, the computer will not work.

- There are multiple types of expansion slots. They are ISA, AGP, and PCI.

Quiz Time!

1. The _____ is the heart of the computer.

   a) Memory

   b) CPU

   c) Hard drive

   d) CD/DVD drive

2. Name 2 things that you can connect to a USB port.

   a) _____

   b) _____

3. RAM gets re-written over and over again

   a) True

   b) False

4. Name 2 types of hard drive connections.

   a) _____

   b) _____

CHAPTER 3

Connecting Your PC

So, your parents bought you a computer and now you are wondering how to connect it all. Well, great news! Everything is color coded. When you buy a new PC and open it up, you will notice that all the devices, such as mouse, keyboard and monitor are usually color coded so you know where to plug them in.

You look at your computer and you say "Wait a minute, there is no color coded connectors on the back of my computer!". The reason being is most likely that you do not have PS/2 connectors. The connections that you have are USB for the mouse and keyboard. This is not unusual and in most cases normal.

The back of a computer may look something like this:

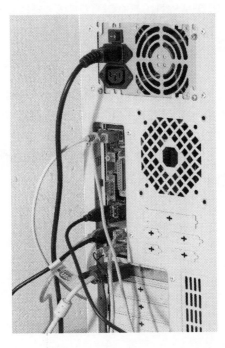

Let's take a closer look at this picture.

- 15 pin video connector color coded as blue.

- Keyboard connector color coded as bright green.

- Mouse connector color coded as purple.

- Speaker connection color coded as mint green.

There are some USB and network connections which are color coded in gray. The network connection looks like a phone jack, except that it is a little wider in size.

The power supply which contains the fan to cool the system and also the power plug to get electricity from the wall jack.

Please note that on the sound card there are usually 3 jacks to plug in other devices. These are usually speakers, a microphone and another device such as a record player so you can record the music that it is playing.

Now let's take a look at your peripherals such as mouse, keyboard and monitor to get started connecting your computer.

Mouse

Keyboard

Network Cable

PC Power Plug

The connectors on the devices are color coded EXACTLY the same way as the back of the computer is. It is done this way purposely so anyone can connect the peripherals and boot up the computer to start using it.

The mouse, keyboard and monitor connections are specific connections and cannot be mistakenly put in the wrong position. If you have a USB mouse and keyboard, it does not matter which USB slot you put these devices in as the computer is smart enough to know that there is one connected and will "auto-detect" them.

Monitor Cable

The monitor has a 15-pin connector which can only go in one way as well. When plugging in the monitor cable, please be careful that you do not bend the pins that are on the cable. If you do, you will find yourself in a bit of trouble. If you have a monitor that the cable is built into it and the pins break or bend, you may find yourself at the closest electronic store picking up a new monitor. If it is a monitor where the cable disconnects from both ends, you can then purchase a new cable.

When connecting your devices to the computer, please plug in the power plug last to ensure that there is no static electricity floating around. This is a safety tip that should be followed regularly.

Always be sure to remove any plastic or protectors covering any slots or ports before installing the devices. By not removing these items, you can damage the port on the computer or bend a pin or two on the actual device.

FUN TIME!

TECHNOLOGY CROSSWORD PUZZLE

INSTRUCTIONS: Look at the list below the puzzle of all the clues that will help you fill in the blanks. You can go back in the book to find the answer.

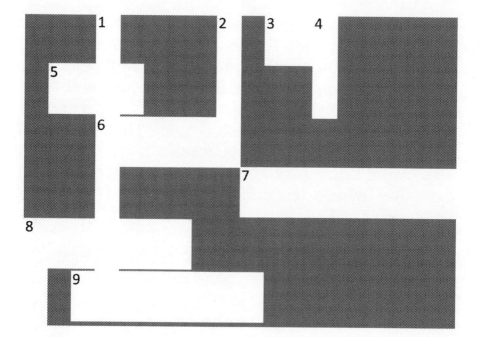

PUZZLE CLUES

ACROSS

3. Short name for Central Processing Unit

5. The color of the network and USB ports.

6. Another name for a computer part.

7. The last thing that you connect to the computer.

8. Has a blue connector on the back of the computer.

9. IS a green PS/2 connector on the back of a computer.

DOWN

1. Can be IDE or SATA.

2. Color of monitor cable connector.

4. A printer gets connected to this type of computer port.

8. Is a purple PS/2 connector on the back of a computer.

SUMMARY:

- Peripheral connections are usually color coded on both sides—the back of the computer and at the end of the cord of the device.

- When connecting the devices to the back of the computer, they can only go in one way. Do not force them in if they don't go in smoothly.

CHAPTER 4

Turning On Your Computer

In this chapter we will get into the steps that the computer takes when you first turn it on. We will also explain some of the choices that you have if you do not want to boot up the computer normally. This would be for troubleshooting purposes.

The Boot Process

So, what does this word "boot" mean? The word boot in computer talk means "to start up". So, booting up the computer means to turn on or start the computer up.

When you first turn on your computer, the first thing that is seen by the system is the power supply. If the power supply is not working properly, the computer will not proceed to boot up.

Next, the power supply gives power to the motherboard which then tries to locate the CPU, memory and other vital components. The most obvious component that you will notice is the video display.

The computer sends out signals to the video card and then translates those signals into pixels which is what you see on the screen. If there is any issue with any of these components, the computer will either do one of two things:

- Give a few beep error codes.

- Display an error message on the screen.

This book will not go into specific error codes. These error codes are known as POST error codes. When you get a POST error code, you will need to do some research on the internet. You should do your research through Google—the search engine of choice. In most cases, you can just enter the actual error code and it will return more than a few results.

At this point in the boot up process, it may be a hardware failure where you may need to swap out a video card or change memory. Providing there are no error messages on boot up, let's proceed to the next step in the process.

After your computer detects the vital components and starts displaying information on the screen, you will see the manufacturer's logo along with some special keys that you can press to get into different modes.

Some of the keys that you may see on this screen are:

- F2 to run Setup

- F12 to see the boot menu

The "F" keys or better known as "function" keys are located at the top of your keyboard. They are labeled as F1, F2, F3, and so on.

F2—Entering Setup

The F2 key is a very powerful key on your computer. If you hit this key while still seeing the manufacturer logo screen, it will say "Entering Setup" in the lower left corner of your screen. When you enter setup, you will be presented with a screen that shows you the basic configuration of the computer. This is known as BIOS.

NOTE: All BIOSes are NOT the same! The wording and the actual features may be different. We will take a general look at some BIOS features. Please keep in mind that this will not be a technical discussion about BIOS, just an introduction.

Let's run through some of the items that are on this screen. You should familiarize yourself with some of these as you may need them when you start to learn how to troubleshoot computer problems.

The first item we will discuss is the "System Info" section. This section provides you with a summary of what is inside the PC. It is a quick rundown of the specs. It will display memory, time and date, video display and other information that you may need to help troubleshoot computer problems. For example, let's say your system was locking up frequently and was giving you error messages about not having enough memory. One of the things that may cause this is a bad memory chip.

You can verify on this screen how much memory the computer sees. If you know that you have 2GB (gigabytes) of physical memory installed in the PC and it is only showing you 1GB then it could mean that you have a memory chip that has gone bad. At this point, you would need to possibly purchase a new memory chip, open up your computer, replace the chip, close your computer and test out the new chip and make sure that the computer sees the new chip. As a note, please make sure that you get the same type of memory that is already installed. If you don't you will probably get some sort of POST error message stating that there is a mismatch. There are many other ways you can use System Info.

The next item on the list would be "Standard Features". In this section, you will find information about what type of hard drives and CD/DVD drives the system sees. You can go into each of these options and modify their values and enable or disable them.

Next, is what I think can help you when your computer doesn't boot up correctly. This section is called "Boot Device Configuration." In this section you will see "Boot Order" or "Boot Priority" menu. This menu allows you to change the boot device on your computer. This can come in handy if your computer doesn't boot and you have a recovery disc. A recovery disc is used to try and back up your files onto a flash drive so you can reinstall Windows. It is sort of a back door into the computer. In this case you would need to change the boot priority so the CD/DVD drive is the first boot option. If you change the boot order within the BIOS, this is more of a permanent change, meaning that every time the computer boots up, it will look in the CD/DVD drive and try to boot. You may not want to do this as this will slightly slow down the boot process. On most computers, if you press the F12 key on your keyboard, this will also bring you into a boot menu where you can temporarily boot off of another device. When you are in the BIOS, in the boot order menu, there are instructions on the bottom of the screen that tell you how to change the boot order. Please make sure you read all screens before making changes.

Other Features:

There are other features of BIOS as well. Some of these features are as follows:

- Load BIOS defaults

- Setting Supervisor Passwords

- Power Management Options

- Integrated Peripheral Configuration

Below you will find a basic description of what these features do. You will need to get familiar with BIOS before attempting to set any of these options. If you set any of these options wrong, it may have undesirable results. For most options there will be a "Confirm" dialog box that pops up to ensure you want to make the changes. At this point, you would choose either Yes or No.

Load BIOS Defaults

This option will reset EVERYTHING in BIOS. This means it will bring the system configuration back to factory settings. This does not mess with any of your files on your hard drive. However, if you do this, error messages may start popping up as it will think certain devices are installed on the system, such as a floppy drive. You will need to go into the BIOS again and disable these options manually.

Setting Supervisor Passwords

This is one of the most deadliest options. Why? If you set a password on the computer and then forget what you typed after you save it, you will not be able to access your computer. Some people put passwords on their computer for security reasons, especially laptop computers. Please be careful when using this option! There is a way to reset the password via the motherboard. It is usually a jumper you take off for a few seconds and then put back on. This "clears" the password.

Power Management Options

These options are used to save energy and do remote wake-up operations. You can set your computer to turn on at a certain time. This comes in handy if you want to turn on your computer 30 minutes before you want to use it.

Integrated Peripheral Configuration

This option is to help configure on-board devices such as network cards and sound cards. One example of how you can use this option is if you purchased a network card and installed it in your computer, you can disable the on-board network card. When we say "on-board", we mean "on the motherboard". These are built in devices that can be configured manually either on or off. This comes in handy when trying to configure and troubleshoot Microsoft Windows problems.

F12—Boot menu

When you press the F12 key on your keyboard on the logo screen for your computer it should bring you into a boot menu screen. On some machines it may be the ESC (Escape) or F9 key. This screen allows you to boot from other devices installed on your PC besides your internal hard drive.

You can boot from a USB device, a network, or the HDD (Hard Disk Drive). In most cases you will also have an option to boot from CD/DVD. The way you choose the boot device is by moving your up and down arrow keys and pressing ENTER on the device that you want to boot from. Most computers use CD or USB as an alternate way to boot.

F8—Advanced Boot Options (The Hidden Key)

This function key is not shown on the logo screen of your computer. You just have to know it is there. This option is more for the advanced computer user. These options are mainly used for troubleshooting your operating system and running other diagnostic tools to help repair your computer. Some of these include doing system restores and running virus scans in what is known as "Safe Mode". Just like BIOS options, you should not mess with these. If you are not sure what an option does, please read your manual.

SUMMARY:

- You can change whatever you want in BIOS. Please make sure that you review all changes before saving them. If you are not sure of a certain option or value, please read the manual that came with your system. On most systems, the F10 key is to save your changes. Pressing the F10 key will prompt the system to confirm your changes.

- When you press F8 while looking at the manufacturer logo screen, this will get you into "diagnostic" mode.

- By pressing F12 will provide you with the boot menu so you can choose between which device you want to boot from.

CHAPTER 5

Microsoft Windows Basics

What is the Microsoft Windows Operating System?

Microsoft Windows is the GUI (pronounced goo-ee)—graphical user interface that you see once your computer boots up. It is also known as the OS or Operating System. The current version of Microsoft Windows as of this book writing is Microsoft Windows 7. There were many different versions of Microsoft Windows in previous years. The very first version that people used was Microsoft Windows 3.1. This version of the OS was on several floppy disks which took about 15-20 minutes to install. Now, with Microsoft Windows 7, it is on a DVD and takes about an hour to install. The reason why it takes longer now is because of the amount of software drivers and service packs that it needs to install. A service pack is nothing more than a group of updates to the operating system. Microsoft releases these service packs as a way to update the system in a quick and easy way. Once you start learning Microsoft Windows and getting to know how to use it, you will perform Microsoft Windows updates on a regular basis to avoid any issues.

Getting to know Microsoft Windows

When you first boot up Microsoft Windows, you will get the Microsoft Windows splash screen. After that, you may be prompted for a username and password. You will need to know this information in order to login to your computer. If there is no username or password you will then be automatically taken to the "desktop.

The desktop may look something like this:

The desktop consists of a few areas that you need to be aware of. They are:

- Start Menu

- Task bar

- Icons

- Wallpaper

The Start Menu

The start menu is probably one of the most common places on the Microsoft Windows desktop that you will use. It almost looks like a menu at a restaurant. You read the menu and pick something. Well, with Microsoft Windows it is the same way. You click on the "START" button which is located at the bottom left of your screen. Sometimes, it will not show the word "start" but instead show a picture of the Microsoft logo. Either way, click once on this and you should get the menu.

As you can probably imagine, there are many options. I will describe some of them here in this section.

All Programs

When you click on "All Programs", you will see a list of just that—all the programs that are installed on your computer. You can then choose a program you want to open and use.

Control Panel

This area is the place where you would configure the operating system settings such as display, network, sound and other settings. This is sort of like the BIOS of the operating system. Please use caution when using any of these settings.

Chris Cataldo

One of the most common areas that you will use is under Programs. You will see a link to "Uninstall A Program". When you click on this link, it will bring up all the programs that the computer sees installed. You can then right click on one and choose "Uninstall". This will remove the application from your system. There are 3rd party programs that you can use later on to further clean up the application. Sometimes, there are entries in the registry and files left on the hard drive. You can download a program called CCleaner. You can find and download it at their official website:

http://www.piriform.com/download

The Control Panel looks something like this:

Documents

This is pretty self explanatory. This is the default folder where Microsoft Windows keeps your documents. You will find all of your documents stored here if you didn't manually choose where to save them. Sometimes this folder can get messy pretty quickly. My recommendation to you is to create separate folders for word processing documents, spreadsheets and other types of documents such as PDF's. You may find yourself scrolling through pages and pages of documents if you do not organize them.

Help and Support

Here you will find a great deal of information if you need it. Microsoft Windows has a built in index which you can search against. It will also pull information from the internet and give you the latest updated information. After you bring up the documentation that you want, you can also print this out instead of reading it on the screen. This can come in handy when you are trying to follow instructions on how to do something within Microsoft Windows.

When you open Help and Support, it should look something like this:

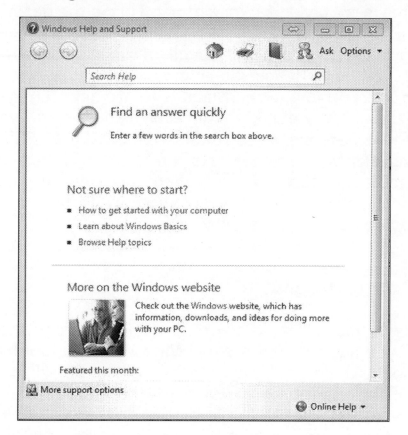

<u>Devices and Printers</u>

If you installed a printer, scanner or any other device you will find it in this section. You can view hard drive files, set printers as default, and add a device to the system. If you are adding a device to the system, such as a printer, you should be sure to have the CD or DVD that came with that device. Microsoft Windows does not detect every single piece of hardware. You do have the option of going online and trying to download the driver software on the manufacturer's website. When doing this, please make sure that you are downloading the software for the correct version of Microsoft Windows. A lot of the driver software out there will run on any version of Micrsoft Windows. It will also support 32-bit and 64-bit machines. If you install the wrong drivers, you may see a BSOD (Blue Screen Of Death). Always make sure that you have your data backed up on a regular basis to an external hard drive or flash drive.

When you open Devices and Printers, it should look like this:

Run

Here you can run commands manually if you know what they are. Advanced computer users can use this for troubleshooting purposes. You can type CMD in order to get to a command line interface to issue your commands or to look for certain files without changing the settings in Microsoft Windows. For example, you can type D:\SETUP to install an application from your DVD drive.

The other way would be to click on Start, click on Computer, then double click on your DVD drive and then finally, double clicking on SETUP.EXE. Why do 4 mouse clicks when you can just type in the command in one simple line? You also have the option to browse to the file on your hard drive and run it like that.

Please note that there are some applications that you may need to run as an administrator. You run programs as the administrator by right clicking on the application and choose "Run as administrator".

The Run dialog box looks like this:

| Run | ☒ |

Type the name of a program, folder, document, or Internet resource, and Windows will open it for you.

Open: [_____] ▼

🛡 This task will be created with administrative privileges.

OK   Cancel   Browse...

Task Bar

The task bar acts as a quick way to get into programs. The task bar also holds the system's date and time in the lower right hand corner of the screen along with programs that start up when the computer first boots up. You can add and delete programs from the task bar through the Quick Launch bar. When you delete the program from the quick launch bar, you do not uninstall the program. All this does is get rid of the icon associated with the program.

The task bar looks like this:

Start | ▪ ▷ 🖳 🔊 | 10:48 AM 8/15/2012 ▪

To add an item to the Quick Launch bar, do the following:

- Click the icon of the program that you want on the quick launch bar.

- Drag the icon down to the quick launch bar.

To remove an item from the Quick Launch bar, do the following:

- Right click on the program that you want to remove on the Quick Launch bar.

- Click on "Unpin this program from the task bar".

Wallpaper

The wallpaper is the area of the screen above the task bar where it usually has a picture of some sort. You can change the wallpaper to pretty much whatever you want. You can also import your own pictures to use as wallpaper. This area of the screen is also known as the desktop.

To change the wallpaper, do the following:

- Click Start

- Click Control Panel

- Click on Change desktop background under Appearance.

You will then be able to choose from solid colors, desktop backgrounds and from the picture gallery.

Icons

These are the pictures that you see on top of your wallpaper. These icons are just "shortcuts" to the actual program that are installed on your PC. You can create your own shortcuts to programs that you may have installed that didn't create one for you. By double clicking your mouse on the icon, you access the program that is associated with the icon.

To create a shortcut on the desktop for a program, do the following:

- Right click on an empty area on the desktop.

- Click on New.

- Click on Shortcut.

- Click on the Browse button to search for the program you want to create the shortcut for.

- Click Next.

- Type a name for the shortcut that you will know what it is.

- Click Finish.

One of the icons on the desktop is called "Recycle Bin". This icon is used to hold the items that you have deleted. When you delete something, you can get it back. Even though you delete stuff from the computer, it goes in this area so you can restore it later if need be. This acts as a safety net for your computer. Once items are deleted from the recycle bin they are permanently gone unless of course you have a backup of your data.

Be aware of the Recycle Bin because if you have a lot of stuff that you have deleted, this can fill up your hard drive after a period of time.

To empty the recycle bin and permanently delete all data, do the following:

- Right click on the Recycle Bin.

- Click on Empty Recycle Bin.

The Recycle Bin looks like this:

__Computer Icon__

The Computer icon when doubled clicked on displays all hard drives, CD/DVD drives, removable drives, such as flash drives and external hard drives, card readers, and networked drives. You will see they are categorized like this. From this screen, you will also see that you can "Uninstall a program", go into "Control Panel", and "Map a network drive". This icon is basically a central point where you can do a lot of different things with using the least amount of clicks of the mouse.

When you open the Computer Icon, it should look like this:

Another feature of this screen is the "Organize" drop down menu at the top left. You will see an option there for "Folder and Search options". If you click on this, you can configure how Microsoft Windows displays files and folders, view hidden items and how to search for items within the folder hierarchy.

The last option I would like to discuss would be the "System Properties" tab. This tab is special because you can do Microsoft Windows Updates and check your computer's hardware in Device Manager.

These screens look like this:

Microsoft Windows Updates are downloaded on a regular basis. Most updates that come out are usually security updates to close the operating system from hackers who try and get into your computer without permission. It is very important to keep up to date with these updates. If you re-format (wipe your hard drive clean), you will need to do all these updates. You may need to run Microsoft Windows updates multiple times before installing any sort of software. Most programs take advantage of the latest updates.

If for some reason Microsoft Windows Updates do not run properly and you get an error message, follow these steps in trying to get it resolved:

- Click Start

- In the Search box, type SERVICES.MSC (no caps needed).

- Scroll down until you see WINDOWS UPDATE.

- Right click on WINDOWS UPDATE and choose "Stop".

- Leaving that window open, Click Start.

- Click Computer.

- Double click your C: drive.

- Double click the WINDOWS folder.

- Double click the SOFTWAREDISTRIBUTION folder.

- Press CTRL key + the A key at the same time. All files and folders should be highlighted in blue.

- Right click on the blue highlighted area and click Delete.

• Go back to the SERVICES.MSC window from step B from above. Right click on WINDOWS UPDATE and choose "Start".

You should now be able to get Microsoft Windows Update running again. If you are still having issues getting this to work, you may need to use available search engines to find solutions for the error message. There are a number of things that would prevent Microsoft Windows Updates from being updated. The PC may contain viruses or the OS (Operating System) may be corrupted.

In Microsoft Windows you can change the icon to whatever you want. For example, if the blue E is not what you want to describe Microsoft Internet Explorer you can change it to a different icon. You can also change the icon properties, meaning if you right click on the icon and choose properties, you can change where and how the program starts and behaves. You can also drag items from the start menu to create shortcuts on the desktop for easy access.

To change a program's icon, do the following:

• Search for the file you want to change the icon for on your C: drive and right click on it. This will most likely be a file on your desktop.

• Click on Properties.

- Click on Change Icon.

- Choose the icon that you want to use and click OK.

The icon should now have changed to the one that you just picked.

SUMMARY

- When you are looking for a program, you should begin by clicking your Start menu. All installed programs will show up there.

- When deleting items from the recycle bin, please make sure that you are sure you want to do that. Once the items are deleted, they are gone forever.

- The Computer icon is a central point where you can do most computer tasks.

- When adding new hardware to your computer, make sure that you have the correct software drivers that go with it.

- When saving a document that you were working on, the computer saves it in the Documents folder on the Start menu. The same is true for any pictures that you save to the default location. When you click start, you will also see a Pictures icon.

CHAPTER 6

Installing and Uninstalling Programs

Installing and Uninstalling programs are a pretty easy process. I will walk you through both here in this section.

Installing Programs and Autoplay

Installing a program in most cases is very easy. We will talk about doing an installation from a CD for right now. When you put a CD in your computer that you bought from the store, a window will pop up with a bunch of different options on it.

The Autoplay screen looks like this:

In most cases you will see an option that says "Run <program name> where <program name is the name of the file that is on the CD that causes you to run the installation. When you click on this option, it will start a wizard that leads you into installing the program.

In most cases when the installation is completed, you will have a button to click on to finish it. Yep, you guessed it! The FINISH button.

As the installation is going, you will see a progress bar going across showing you the percentage that it has completed.

Now, verify that your program is installed correctly. Please do the following steps:

- Click Start

- Click Control Panel

- Click on View By in the upper right hand corner and choose "Small icons".

- Click on Programs and Features

- You should now see a list of programs that come up in alphabetical order. You should be able to look at this list and find your program that you just installed.

Once you have verified that the program is installed, you can click on the X in the upper right hand corner of the Programs and Features box to close the dialog box.

Uninstalling a program from your computer

Uninstalling a program is even simpler. Here are the steps to uninstall a program.

- Click Start.

- Click Control Panel.

- Click View By in the upper right hand corner and click "Small Icons".

- Click Programs and Features.

- Highlight the program you want to uninstall and right click on it.

- Click "Uninstall".

- Follow the uninstall wizard that comes up on the screen until it prompts you to click the Finish button.

Note that some programs require a reboot after uninstall. Screens are similar for install and uninstall. Please make sure that you do not uninstall any programs that are required by the operating system. Some of these programs are .NET Framework, Java and Adobe Flash players.

CHAPTER 7

Common Programs on Your Computer

Now that you know how to install and uninstall programs, let's look at how to open them. To access the programs that are installed on the computer, please do the following:

- Click Start.

- Click All Programs.

- Click the program that you want to open.

You may see programs that are listed as folders. It may look like this:

Microsoft Office
- Microsoft Office Access 2007
- Microsoft Office Excel 2007
- Microsoft Office Groove 2007
- Microsoft Office InfoPath 2007
- Microsoft Office OneNote 2007
- Microsoft Office Outlook 2007
- Microsoft Office PowerPoint 2007
- Microsoft Office Publisher 2007
- Microsoft Office Word 2007
- Microsoft Office Tools

So if you wanted Microsoft Excel 2010, you would have to click on that and not just the Microsoft Office folder.

Now that you know how to get to the programs, let's browse around and talk about some of the most common programs on your computer.

Some of the programs that we will discuss here are:

- Calculator

- Notepad

- Paint

- Microsoft Windows Explorer

These programs are built into Microsoft Windows, so there is no need to install anything. These programs are also under the "Accessories" section under "All Programs" so you don't have to try and figure out where they are on your computer.

Shall we get started? Ok, Great!

Calculator

Let's go and try and open up the Calculator program. To do this, follow these few steps:

- Click Start

- Click All Programs

- Click Accessories

- Click Calculator

The calculator will look something like this:

Look at the top of the calculator. You see View, Edit and Help. This is what's known as the "menu bar". Make sure you get familiar with this because just about every single program you open will have this.

This is used as a navigation tool to help you use the program. On a lot of other programs you will see File, Edit, View, Tools, and Help.

You can use the calculator to add, subtract, multiply and divide numbers without your traditional pen and paper and making a mistake. This can come in handy when doing math questions for homework if your teacher allows you to use it.

If you click on the View option, you will see there are different calculators that you can use. You use your mouse to click the buttons on the calculator to display in the little window.

Practice using the calculator for 10 minutes and then move on with this chapter.

Notepad

Notepad is a small text editor where you can write text and then save it for future use. This can come in handy if you are on the phone with someone who tells you to jot down their email address and you don't have any pen and paper. You can open Notepad, type your text and then save it to your desktop.

To open Notepad, please do the following:

- Click Start.

- Click All Programs.

- Click Accessories.

- Click Notepad.

Notepad looks something like this:

In notepad you can change fonts and sizes of text you write. You will see that if you click on the "Format" menu option and choose "Font". Notice the "Size" field. The lowest font size is 8 and the highest is 72. The average font size is 12 for most documents, whether you use notepad or another word processing program such as Microsoft Word. After you type in your text, including fonts and font sizes, you can click on "File" and then "Save". Notepad will then prompt you to save the file on your hard drive. The default location is the "Documents" folder.

Note that when you first open notepad it shows on the top bar as "Untitled". This is normal until you save it and give it a name. The name of the file can be any name you want to give it. No special characters in the name, just letters and numbers.

Practice typing in a few sentences and changing some of the fonts and sizes. Then save the file and try to open it.

Paint

Paint is a drawing program built into Microsoft Windows. To access paint, please do the following:

- Click Start.

- Click All Programs.

- Click Accessories.

- Click Paint.

Paint looks something like this:

With Microsoft Paint you can create and edit pictures. The program teaches you the basics of drawing and painting using computer software.

Some of the tools in Microsoft Paint are as follows:

- Pencil tool.

- Magnifier tool.

- Eraser tool.

- Text tool.

- Brush tool.

These are just some of the common tools that you can use to create and edit pictures. There is plenty of information online on how to use them.

Microsoft Windows Explorer

Microsoft Windows Explorer is a tool where you can do so many different things. Some of the things you can do are:

- Open up a drive's contents and view it.

- Map network drives to your computer.

- Check system properties.

- Uninstall or change a program.

- Open control panel

- Copy, Paste and Cut Files and Folders.

- Create folders and subfolders.

- Delete files and folders.

In order to access Microsoft Windows Explorer:

- Click Start

- Right click on Computer

- Click on Open.

Once this opens, you will see your hard drive, CD/ DVD drive, memory card readers and any other drives, including but not limited to external hard drives, cell phones and printer storage.

Microsoft Windows Explorer looks like this:

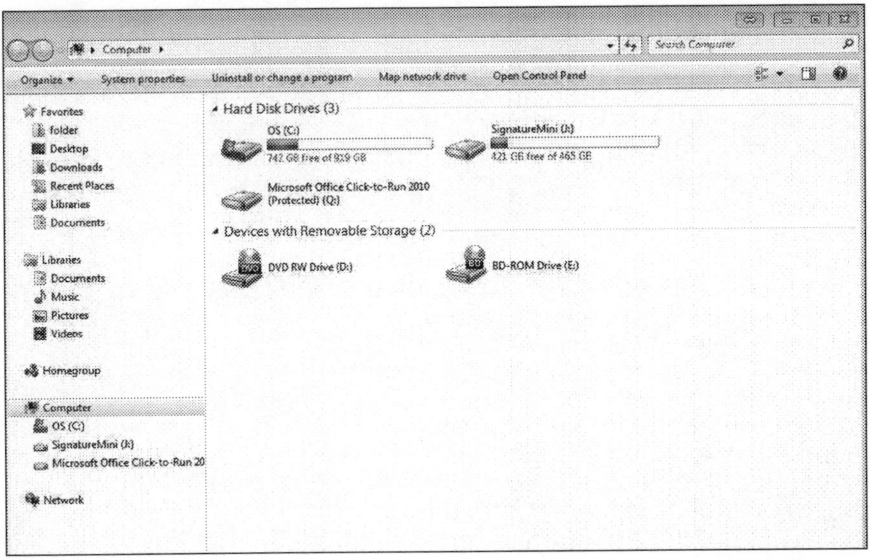

<u>SUMMARY</u>

- Notepad is a Microsoft Windows application that you write some basic text and save it for future use.

- Paint is used to draw pictures.

- Microsoft Windows Explorer lets you do many different things. It is the central point

CHAPTER 8

Microsoft Internet Explorer Basics

Microsoft Internet Explorer is yet another program on your computer. This is a special kind of program. This is called a browser. You request information through the browser. The browser then goes out to the internet, grabs the data you requested and displays it on the screen.

Another special thing about Microsoft Internet Explorer is that most times it will sit in the task bar next to the start menu for easy access.

You can also get to the browser by going through the start menu. The steps to take to open the browser from the start menu are as follows:

- Click Start

- Click All Programs

- Click Internet Explorer

This will look something like this:

We will discuss some of the items that you will see in the browser program. The following items are all part of the browser:

- Address bar

- Status bar

- Other toolbars

- Viewing window

- Navigational buttons

Ok so let us begin our journey through the browser. This will just be an introduction about the browser itself and no technical discussions about error messages or the like.

Go ahead and open up your browser on your computer so you can follow along.

Navigational Buttons

In the upper left corner of the browser you will see two arrows. One arrow is pointing to the left and one is pointing to the right. They look like the following:

These arrows let you move between web pages easily and quickly. They represent backwards and forwards.

Address Bar

The address bar is to the right of the navigation button on the top of the Microsoft Internet Explorer window. It will have something in the address bar that may look similar to this:

<u>http://www.techservicestation.com</u>

This is what is known as a web address. There is a lot to know about web addresses and how they are formed, but we will keep it very simple here. A web address is nothing more than a placeholder on the internet for a person or business. You can access millions of websites planet-wide. A good thing about websites is that the name of the website usually represents the person or business. For example, if you were looking for toys, you may want to try and go to the following website:

<u>http://www.abctoys.com</u>

Toolbars

Toolbars are small programs added to the browser. They help you with other types of activities that you may want to do while on the internet. There are a few different types of toolbars. Here they are:

- Favorites toolbar.

- Search toolbars.

Favorites Toolbar

The favorites toolbar is right below the menu bar. It is the bar that has the star icon:

You can click this icon to add the current webpage to your favorites so you can access it easily the next time you want to go to that web page.

Search Toolbars

Generally speaking I do not like search toolbars as they can slow down your browsing experience, however, for computer beginners, it can help in searching for what you want online without going to a separate web page just to do the search.

You can have the Google toolbar at the top of the browser. By having this toolbar there, you do not need to go to http://www.google.com. You can type your search right in the toolbar and get your results as if you had gone to the actual Google web site.

CAUTION: You do not want to have more than one or two toolbars as this will slow down your browser and create all sorts of other issues which may include viruses and performance issues.

A word of advice is to keep your browser as clean as possible at all times to avoid problems.

Status Bar

This bar is located below the viewing window and is an informational bar regarding the web page you are trying to connect to. There are different status messages that can be displayed but the one we are concerned with in this book is the "Done" message. This message basically means that the webpage loaded without any problems and that it is ready for viewing.

Other Features You Can Do Within Microsoft Internet Explorer

Printing

Let's suppose you are on the internet to get directions to drive somewhere and obviously you can't look at your computer while you drive, so you would like to print out a copy of the directions so someone else in the car can read them to you.

To print a web page in Microsoft Internet Explorer, do the following:

- Click File.

- Click Print.

- Choose your printer that you want to print to.

- Click OK.

The menu that is explained above looks like this:

File	Edit	View	Favorites	Tools
New tab				Ctrl+T
Duplicate tab				Ctrl+K
New window				Ctrl+N
New session				
Open...				Ctrl+O
Edit				
Save				
Save as...				Ctrl+S
Close tab				Ctrl+W
Page setup...				
Print...				Ctrl+P
Print preview...				
Send				▶
Import and export...				
Properties				
Work offline				
Exit				

You must have a printer connected and set up in Microsoft Windows in order to print anything. If you click Print and there are no printers set up in

Microsoft Windows, you will not see any printers listed in the print dialog box.

Also, make sure that you have the printer on and ready to be printed to. If it is not ready, you will get error messages as well.

Sending a website to a friend or family member

There are a few ways to send a webpage to someone. We will cover two ways of doing this. They are:

- Page by email.

- Link by email.v

What is the difference you ask? It's actually pretty simple.

The option to send the page by email sends just that—the entire page. This includes pictures. If the person you are sending it to has a slow internet connection, you may just want to send them the link to the page so they don't have to wait for the email to finish loading. They can just click on the link that you sent them and it will open the webpage for them. We will show you step by step how to accomplish this within the browser.

Please keep in mind that when you send an email, no matter what type of email it is, it can be viewed by anyone at any given time. There is NO PRIVACY!

To send a webpage by email as a link do the following:

- Click File.

- Click Send.

- Click Link by Email.

- Your email program will open up and fill out the subject and the body of the email. All you need to do is fill out the email address who you are sending it to.

- Click Send within your email program. This will send the email.

The screen will look something like this:

Chris Cataldo

To send a webpage by email as a full webpage, you follow the steps above. The only difference is that the actual web page will be in the body of the email and not just the link. So, instead of choosing "Link by email", you choose "Page by email".

Please be aware that some web pages may not show properly in an email due to the size and graphics. Sometimes, it just may be better if you send the link.

SUMMARY:

- You can add websites to your "Favorites" list by clicking on the star icon and accessing them easily.

- Use the right and left arrows to navigate through the web pages that you have visited during the current browsing session.

- By using "search bars" you can get search results a bit faster than if you went to the search engine itself.

- There are 2 ways to send websites to people you know—"Page by email" and "Link by email".

- You can also print websites by using the Print option from the File menu.

CHAPTER 9

Turning Off Your PC

Turning Off Your Computer—
The Right Way!

Turning off your computer correctly is one of the most important things to know about your computer. Unfortunately, there are a lot of people who just turn the computer off with the power button. This is a big no-no.

Here is how you should always turn off your computer:

- Click Start.

- Click Shut Down.

The computer will close any and all programs that you had open. It is recommended that you save your work before shutting down as you will lose all your work once the computer is turned off. Also by turning off the computer with the power button doesn't give Microsoft Windows a chance to close everything and you may end up corrupting Microsoft Windows. There are some tools that can help in repairing these types of situations. Once the computer is off, turn off your monitor, speakers and any other devices that you were using when your computer was up and running.

When Microsoft Windows shuts down, you should see a screen that looks like this:

The computer will take about 30 seconds to a minute to fully shutdown. The only time you should shut the PC down with the power button is if the computer doesn't shut down and appears hung after 5 minutes after you hit "Shut down" from the Start menu.

Also be sure that when you do shut off your PC, it is not running Microsoft Windows updates. Sometimes the system will run updates on logoff/shutdown. If this does come up, please let the updates finish and have Microsoft Windows shut itself down.

Another important thing to mention is, if you have any external devices such as a flash drive or an external hard drive, that you may be using for data backup, please disconnect these devices in a safe way. At the bottom right hand corner of your screen you should see an icon that, if you put your mouse over it, it should say "Safely Remove Hardware". If you right click on this icon, it will display all the USB devices that are connected. Highlight your device that you want to disconnect and then left click it to "eject" it.

About The Author

I started with computers at the early age of 13 when the Atari 400/800 was the computers at the time. I was able to work when I was 14. I saved up my own money and was able to purchase Microsoft Basic the following year. I then started programming and caught on to it and liked it. This led to other programming languages. When I was 19, I landed my first job using mainframes. At the time, I had also done business application programming. After that, I moved on to helpdesk positions supporting all versions of Microsoft Windows and Windows-based applications. I have also worked on AS/400 systems both as a security officer and administrator. Currently, as of this writing, (July 2012), I am a level 3 technician/backup team lead for one of the largest insurance companies in the world. During the past 10 years I have also gained industry standard certifications from Microsoft and other leading companies.

Contact The Author Directly

You may contact me directly with any questions, comments, or suggestions for future publications.

Email: chris@kidscomputerbooks.com

Website: www.kidscomputerbooks.com

Phone: 917-913-7808 (Voice Mail Available). Please allow up to 72 hours for a response.

<u>NOTE TO PARENTS</u>

I offer personal training sessions for your child. In order to help the child understand the material, it is highly recommended that they get at least 3 sessions a week. My rates are very reasonable. Each session lasts 1 hour. Sessions include teaching and hands-on where your child can practice what was taught. You may contact me through the information above if your child is interested.

LAST COMMENTS FROM THE AUTHOR

I hope you enjoyed reading this book. I hope it has inspired you to learn the computer and learn as much as you can. Computers run our everyday lives and are usually people friendly. Starting out young like you are gives you a basic but yet strong fundamental approach to the computer industry and how it works. As you will see as you go along, reading this book was a major building block in getting started. I was 13 years old when I first started with computers. I have taught children in your age group and even a little younger on how to work the computer.

As a last note, I hope you enjoyed reading this book and hopefully there will be more advanced books to come.